SOON after the Battle of Hastings the Normans built a castle at Rochester to guard the point where the Roman road of Watling Street (the present A2) crossed the River Medway. As the lowest bridge-point of the Medway, Rochester controlled communications by road and water. The Romans established a town there, which was later walled. Much of this still existed in the late eleventh century.

The first temporary castle was almost certainly built within the area of the Roman town, probably on the site of the present castle. It would have been defended by a wall of timber and earth, and surrounded by a deep ditch. This castle was one of the earliest in England to be rebuilt in stone. Work was begun in about 1087-88 by Gundulf, Bishop of Rochester. He was famous as being 'very competent and skilful at building in stone,' and was also responsible for the Tower of London and the original Rochester Cathedral. His curtain (perimeter) walls still largely delineate the castle's boundaries.

The keep (great tower) was built by William de Corbeil, Archbishop of Canterbury, to whom Henry I granted custody of the castle in 1127. Rochester Castle remained under the authority of the Archbishops of Canterbury until 1215, when it was taken over by the Crown after a seven-week siege by King John. Its size and strategic position made it an important royal stronghold for several hundred years.

Like many older castles, Rochester was abandoned in late medieval times. By the sixteenth century it was falling into decay; it deteriorated further after James I sold it into private hands in 1610. Towards the end of the nineteenth century the estate was bought by Rochester Corporation. In 1965 responsibility for the castle passed to the Ministry of Public Building and Works (later the Department of the Environment). Since 1984 it has been in the care of English Heritage.

Seal of the City of Rochester (both sides) This magnificent example of a medieval seal has been dated to the early thirteenth century

Tour of the Keep

The bold letters in the following paragraphs refer to those on the marginal plans

The keep

The great keep of Rochester Castle is one of the largest in England. It is about 70ft (21m) square, with walls up to 12ft (3.5m) thick and 113ft (34.5m) high to the top of the battlements. Like much of the curtain wall it is made of ashlar or Kentish ragstone with a core of rubble. It is a typical Norman keep of its period, square and massive, with the entrance at first-floor level protected by a forebuilding.

Forebuilding

The ticket office is situated in what was the castle's entrance chamber. This was a good-sized room designed to impress visitors with its great doors, fine double windows, decorated Norman arches and ornate stonework. This chamber and the chapel above are in the forebuilding to the keep.

Imagine the difficulties facing those trying to break into the keep. Originally there were no doorways at ground level so attackers had to come up the outer staircase, itself only 8ft (2.4m) wide, under fire from missiles dropped on them from the battlements. First they would have to take the now-vanished guard tower at the northwest corner of the keep. Further on the drawbridge would be raised, leaving a pit 9ft (2.7m) wide and 15ft (4.6m) deep just in front of the entrance to the fore-building. The raised drawbridge would cover the door itself, and both would have to be broken down before entry could be gained to the forebuilding. Even if they managed to do this, the attackers would still have to break into the keep itself.

Go through the doorway (A on the plan) on to the first-floor viewing platform in the keep This was another very strong door. On either side can be seen the vertical grooves down which a portcullis could be lowered in an emergency. On the inside are large holes for bars to secure the door and side recesses for keys or lanterns.

First floor and entrance chamber

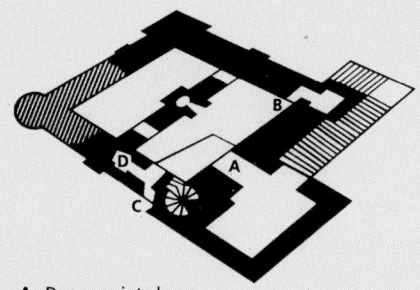

A Doorway into keep
B Gundulf's Chamber
C Postern door
D Ventilated garderobe

Decorated column and arch A capital at the top of a column and chevron decorations on the arch between the forebuilding and the keep

The keep seen from the tower of Rochester Cathedral

TOUR OF THE KEEP

The well shaft could be reached from all floors. This shows how water may have been winched up.

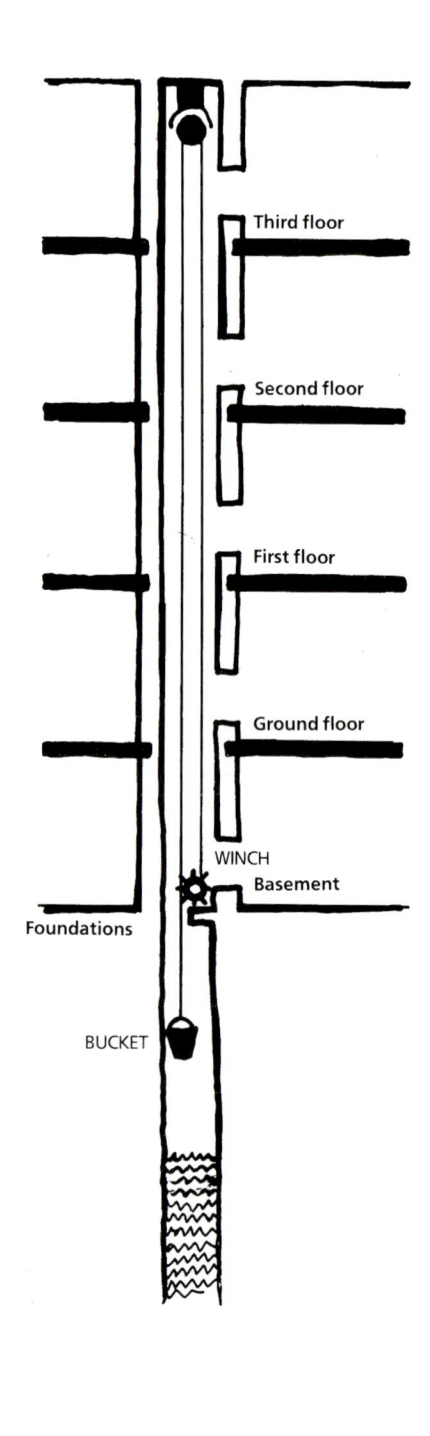

- Third floor
- Second floor
- First floor
- Ground floor
- WINCH — Basement
- Foundations
- BUCKET

Well head at first-floor level, rebuilt in 1826

4

TOUR OF THE KEEP

First floor

This was an important floor with large fireplaces and several garderobes (latrines). The small windows show that the emphasis was still on defence. It would have been a very busy place, assigned to the resident constable to receive visitors, conduct estate business and hold local courts.

In the northwest corner (on the right as seen from the viewing platform) is the entrance to 'Gundulf's Chamber' **B**, once part of a two-roomed apartment that connected with the outer guard tower and may have been the constable's sleeping quarters.

Up a few steps on the left is a small postern door **C** with bolt holes on the inside. To the right of this is a ventilated garderobe **D** which discharged down the wall outside.

Looking up from the viewing platform one can see how the castle was constructed. The strong cross wall gives rigidity to the structure, divided each floor into two separate main rooms and provided a central support for the roof. The lines of holes for floor joists show three storeys above the basement. Stairways in the northeast and southwest turrets led to all floors; only the northeast one can now be used.

The well shaft in the cross wall was accessible at every floor level. It is 65ft (20m) deep from the coping and still contains water. The date 1826 on the well head is the year of its restoration by the Earl of Jersey, whose crest also appears.

Fireplaces can be seen on every floor in the north and south walls, with flues slanting through to vents on the outside instead of chimneys. On the higher residential floors, where defensive considerations could be relaxed, window apertures become bigger and decoration is more ornate.

Descend the steps to the lower viewing platform

First floor and entrance chamber

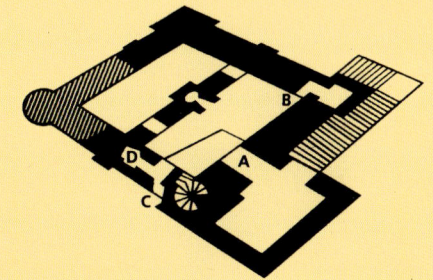

A Doorway into keep
B Gundulf's Chamber
C Postern door
D Ventilated garderobe

Fireplace in the Chamber on the top floor of the keep. Below this are holes for the joists that supported the floor. There are fireplaces on all floors; some of the vents through the outside wall can be seen

Inside Rochester Castle

- First floor
- Second floor
- Mural Gallery
- Third floor
- Battlements and wallwalk

Semicircular tower The curved wall of this tower was intended to deflect missiles. The tower was built to close the breach in the castle enclosure, made by King John's miners during the siege of 1215, and to strengthen a vulnerable position

Fireplaces There are fireplaces on all floors – note the size of them. They all had a smoke vent through the outside wall

Mural gallery Running around the keep at the upper level of the Great Hall, the mural gallery was probably used by minstrels on special occasions and may also have been used as a place for exercise during bad weather and even for extra sleeping space

Chapel

Spiral staircases The two staircases in opposite corners of the keep are spiral and thus economical of space. Only one can now be used

Thick walls The walls are about 12ft (3.7m) thick at the base of the keep and about 10ft (3m) thick at the top. This made it an immensely strong structure and the mural gallery and several mural chambers could be built within the wall

The battlemented wallwalk and towers gave protection to soldiers and had openings for shooting arrows through and dropping missiles on to the enemy. Wooden hoards used when attacking the enemy if they managed to reach the base of the keep are shown on page 12

Roof The roof, in the shape of an M, had guttering for rainwater

Wallwalk This was patrolled to survey the surrounding countryside. The height of the keep, 113ft (34.5m), makes this an excellent vantage point

Decorated arches Note the typical Norman chevron decoration

The well The well shaft rises through the centre of the keep; it was accessible from all floors. How water may have been raised is shown on page 4

Guard tower This no longer exists but traces of it can be seen in the northwest corner of the keep. It was the first line of defence against anyone trying to gain entry to the keep

Forebuilding The purpose of this was to protect the entrance to the keep. It was itself protected by a guard tower, a drawbridge and a pit 9ft wide and 15ft deep (2.7 by 4.6m). A portcullis that could be lowered between the forebuilding and the keep gave additional protection

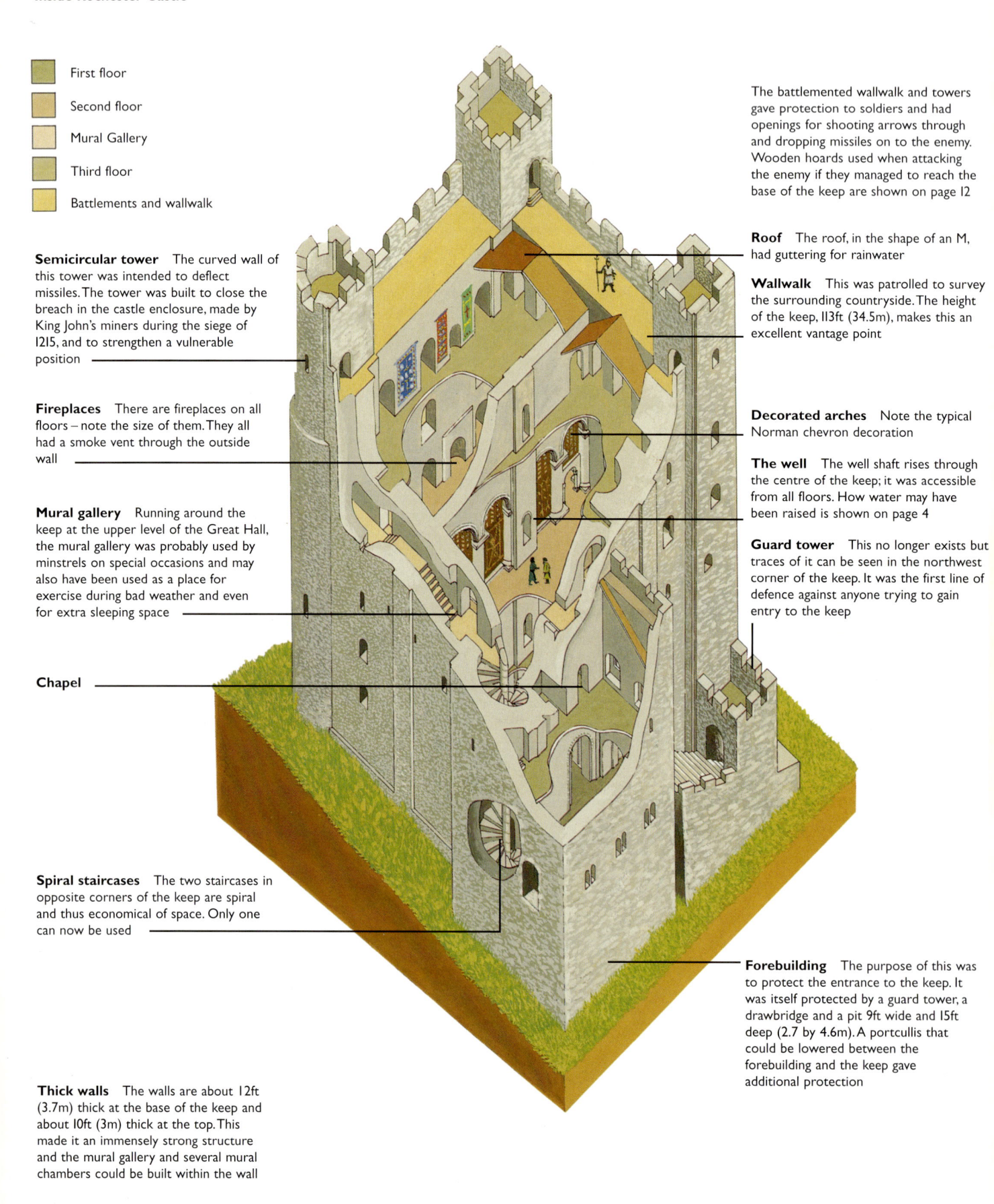

TOUR OF THE KEEP

Basement

This area would have been the castle's storerooms. The sole access was from the floor above, down the northeast stairs. The original earth floor was much higher, about level with the modern wooden platform and corresponding with ground level outside. It was dug out in the early twentieth century to expose the depth of the foundations.

Note the massively thick walls and the absence of windows, except for a few tiny ventilation holes, as a protection against attack from outside. The recesses in the walls were possibly for storing things such as spices or valuables. Notice also the two fissures **E** showing where a quarter of the keep was destroyed in King John's siege (see pages 12, 18 and 25). These may show better when seen from the battlements and outside.

Basement of forebuilding F

This gloomy room is now used as a store and is not open to the public. It was once thought to be a dungeon, but this is unlikely as prisoners were valuable commodities for ransom and were usually kept in healthier, more pleasant chambers. Nevertheless, the room does have the luxury of a private garderobe. Probably it was used as accommodation or for extra storage of valuable goods.

Descend the steps into the sub-basement of the forebuilding To the right is a cesspit for the garderobe which discharged from the aperture above. This must have been the most nauseating place in the castle - pitch black and evil smelling. When the castle was first built the doorway in the outer wall would not have existed, and the only ventilation would have been through the tiny air vent still to be seen above this door.

Go back the way you came and ascend to the second floor A short way up on the left a flight of steps leads into what was the castle's chapel **G**. These were cut through later for more convenient access, destroying the sedilia (priests' seats) to the right of the altar.

As was customary, the chapel was located in the forebuilding over the castle's main entrance. It is still a handsome room with fine windows, and half-octagonal vaulting above the repaved stone floor at the altar end; the timber floor is modern.

The original way in from the keep was through the round-headed doorway **H**. Just outside this can be seen a slot in the floor for the portcullis that protected the main door below. Recesses on either side of the passage may have been for the windlass that raised and lowered the portcullis.

Basement
Sub-basement

E Fissures in wall from 1215 siege
F Basement of forebuilding

Spiral staircase showing the vaulted roof and the doorway through to the chapel

Adrian Field

Second floor and Great Hall

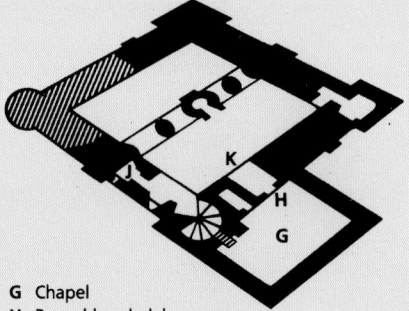

G Chapel
H Round-headed doorway
J Garderobe
K Original entrance vestibule to chapel

TOUR OF THE KEEP

Second floor and Great Hall

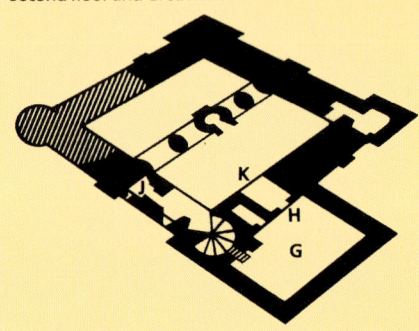

G Chapel
H Round-headed doorway
J Garderobe
K Original entrance vestibule to chapel

Second floor

From the next angle of the stairway, view the Great Hall. This was a fine lofty room 32ft (10m) high. It was lit by two tiers of windows, the larger ones piercing a mural gallery or walkway that encircled the upper part within the thickness of the walls.

The layout of this floor was much grander and more spacious than elsewhere. The solid cross wall was replaced by open columns supporting richly patterned arches that led to the Great Chamber beyond. Elaborate finishing details round the fireplaces, doors and windows show that this was the principal floor, possibly the state apartment of the archbishop.

Note the stone window seats, the greater number of mural chambers for extra privacy, and several garderobes (one is visible at **J** a few feet away to the left).

The first opening on the right in the north wall **K** was the original entrance vestibule to the chapel.

Below: **Great Hall and Chamber** of the principal suite in the keep

Right: **Remains of doorway** that connected the Great Hall and Chamber. The larger arch would have been filled in with a wooden screen

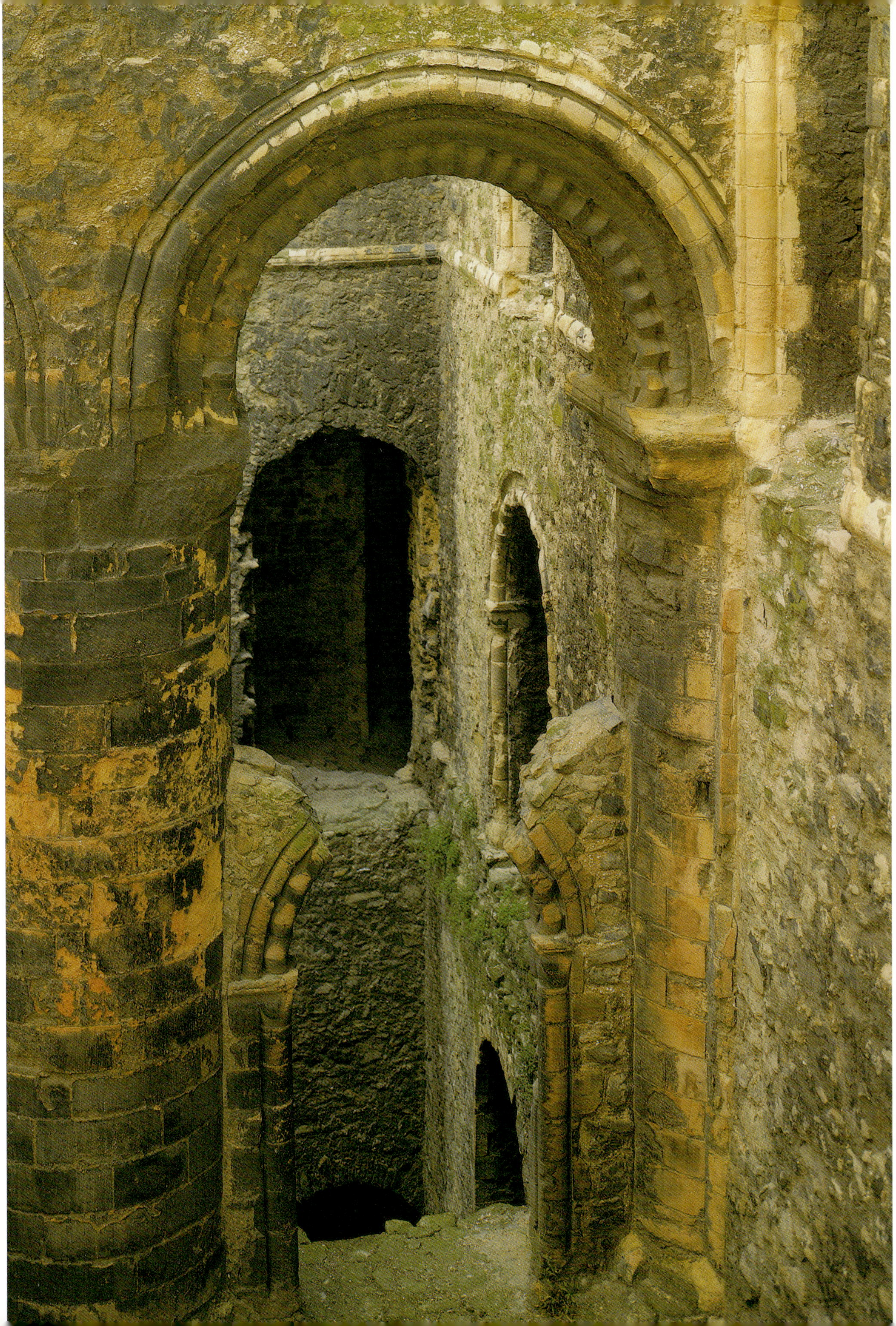

Mural gallery

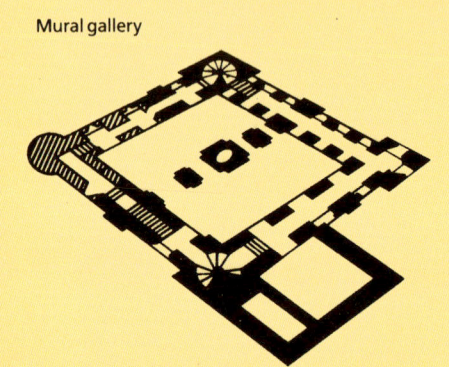

Ascend to the mural gallery This surrounded the upper half of the Great Hall and looked down into it. The gallery might have been used for exercise during unpleasant weather, for minstrels on festive occasions, and may even have provided extra sleeping space when needed. The outer window apertures are the largest in the castle. The bolt holes of the shutters are still visible in places.

It is worth walking all the way round the gallery and looking down into the interior of the keep. From here one obtains the best view of the decorated arches between the Great Hall and Chamber. The pink patches on the walls and the spatters of lead that can be seen in good light show where the keep was burnt out at some unknown date in post-medieval times.

Return to the northeast stairs and ascend towards the third floor Part way up you will pass a narrow arch **L** on the left which gave access to the battlemented top of the forebuilding.

Third floor

This was another ornate apartment, only slightly less grand than the floor below. Handsome windows in the west wall gave fine views over the river. This floor may have been a kind of penthouse flat for the Archbishops of Canterbury who had custody of the castle until 1215.

Ascend towards the battlements Part way up on the left note a low chamber with a barrel-vaulted roof and a large window overlooking the cathedral.

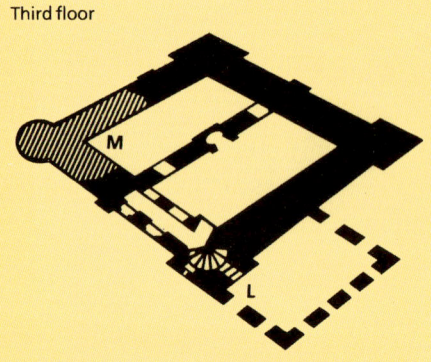

Third floor

L Arch which led on to forebuilding battlements
M Broken arches from 1215 siege

Battlements of the wallwalk and the forebuilding below

Right: **Mural gallery** round the Great Hall and Chamber of the principal suite

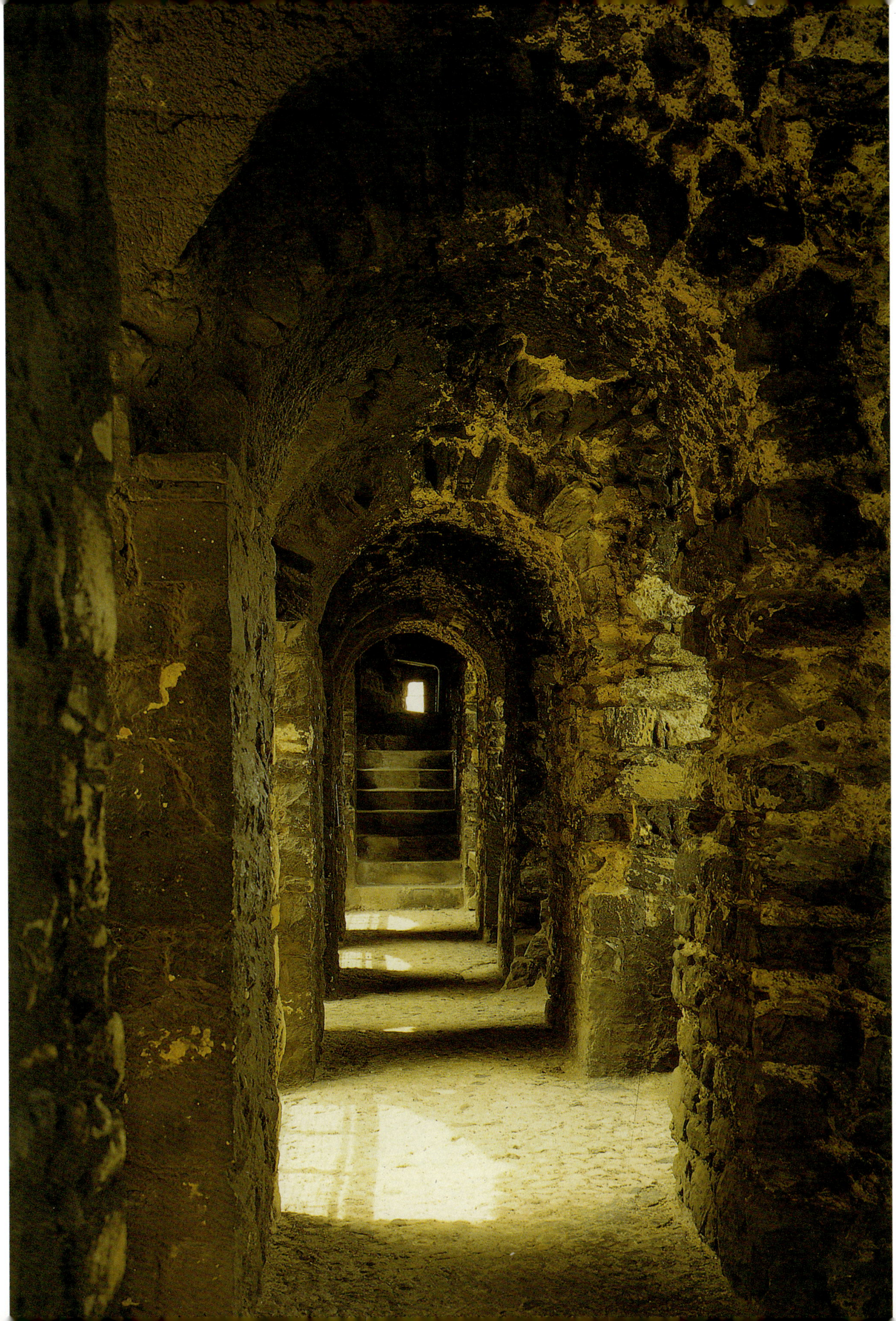

TOUR OF THE KEEP

Battlements

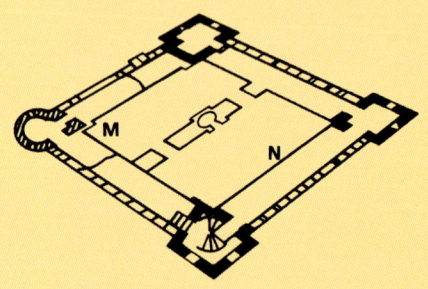

M Broken arches from 1215 siege
N Holes for pigeons and doves that were kept for food

Timber hoards that could be erected in time of war

Roof line of one of the four slopes of the roof

Battlements and wallwalk

By the time you reach the battlements you will have climbed about 150 steps.

At the foot of the outer parapet are holes for the joists of hoards (projecting roofed timber platforms) that could be put out and used for dropping missiles on anyone attacking the base of the keep.

Seashells can be seen embedded in the walls in many places in the castle, but especially around the battlements. These were gathered up with the sand and lime when making the mortar.

Look down on the two large broken arches M between which the whole corner of the keep was brought down. The rebuilt section is noticeably cruder than the original and there are no joist holes.

Near the top of the interior of the east and west walls are traces of the roof line, a shallow M-shape with the cross wall supporting the middle. On the inside of the north wall, just below the top but above the roof line, are a double row of holes N for the pigeons and doves that were kept for food.

Top: **Partly blocked arch** of the archbishop's oratory on the top floor

Right: **The wallwalk** at the top of the keep commands a fine view over the surrounding countryside

12

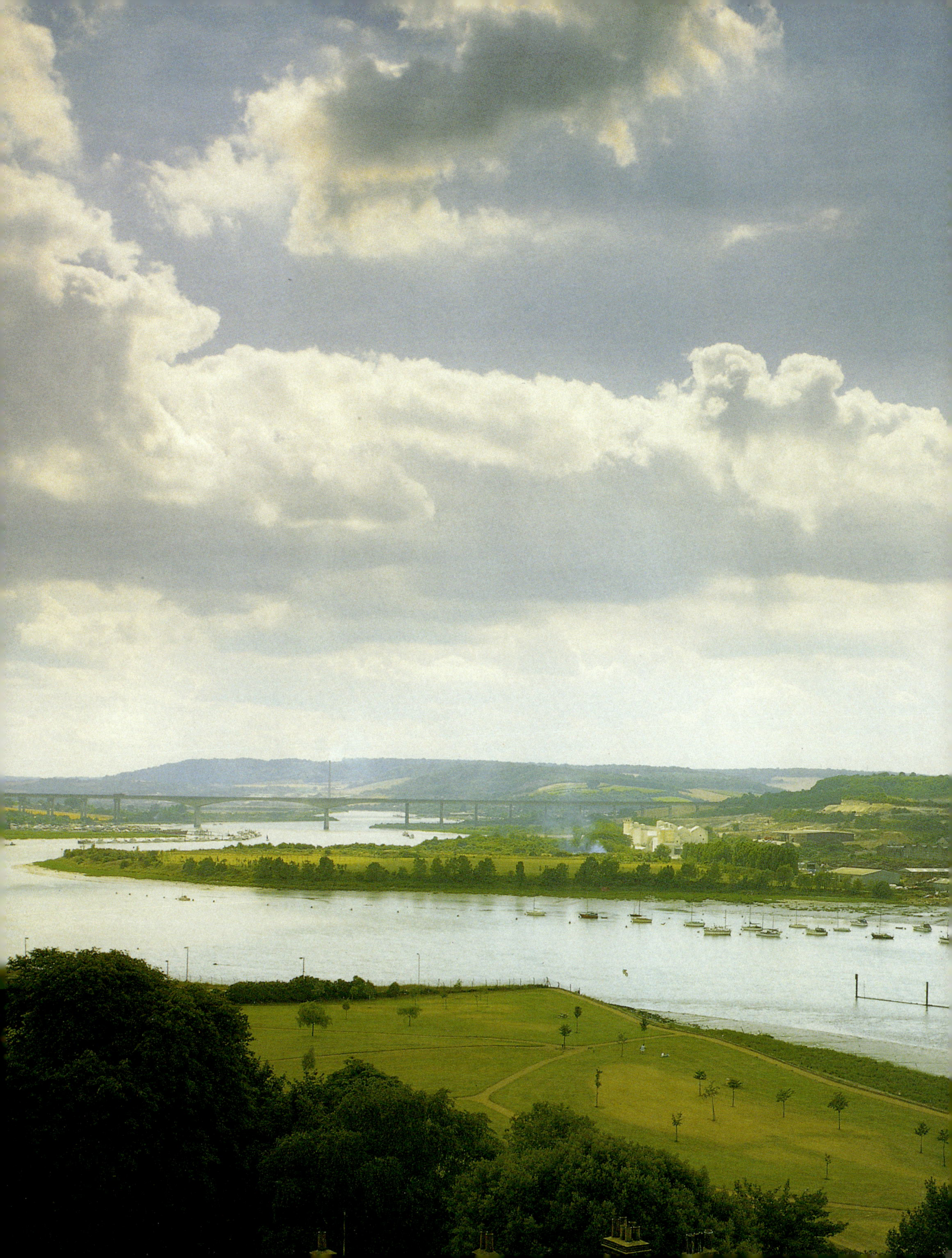

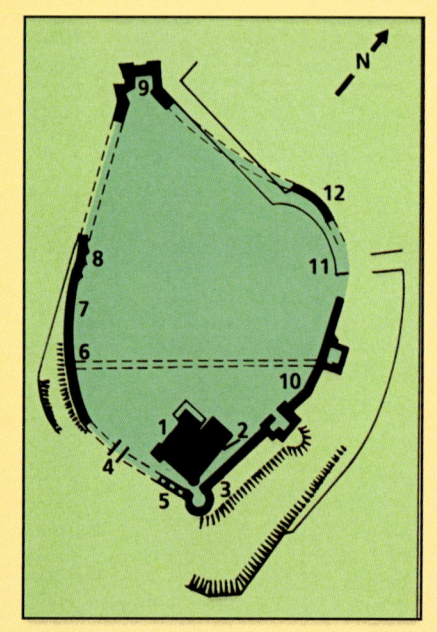

1 The keep
2 Postern door
3 Two-storey drum tower
4 Gate into bailey
5 South curtain wall
6 Embrasures in wall
7 River wall
8 Remnants of thirteenth-century building
9 Northwest bastion
10 Wall built by Edward III
11 Main outer gate
12 Part of Gundulf's wall

Exterior of the drum tower built by Henry III on the southeast corner of the bailey

Far right: **Interior of the drum tower,** note the splayed arrow slits also shown in the inset seen from above

Tour of the bailey

The numbers in the following paragraphs refer to those on the marginal plans

1 From the bailey consider the problems facing anyone attacking the keep. Just below the battlements is the line of joist holes for the wooden hoards from which any of the enemy who reached the base of the tower could be attacked. Windows near the ground are few and narrow, becoming larger only when out of reach of scaling ladders.

   Originally there were no entrances at ground level (the present two in the north wall were cut through much later). The only way in was on the first floor, protected by a strong forebuilding. An assault up the outside staircase would be covered from above. On the steps at the northwest angle of the keep remain traces of a small guard tower that would have had to be taken. The drawbridge would have been raised, leaving a pit just in front of the forebuilding.

2 The small postern door in the east wall of the keep at first-floor level once opened on to a timber bridge to the outer walls. The two downward-sloping chutes to its left are the outlets of garderobes that discharged down the walls. Note the fissure down the middle of the keep; everything to the left of this was brought down by King John's sappers in 1215.

3 The two-storey drum tower was built soon after 1220 to cover the castle's south wall and gate; it may have replaced an earlier tower on the same site. Like the rebuilt corner of the keep behind, it was made cylindrical in shape to deflect missiles and, it was hoped, to be less vulnerable to mining.

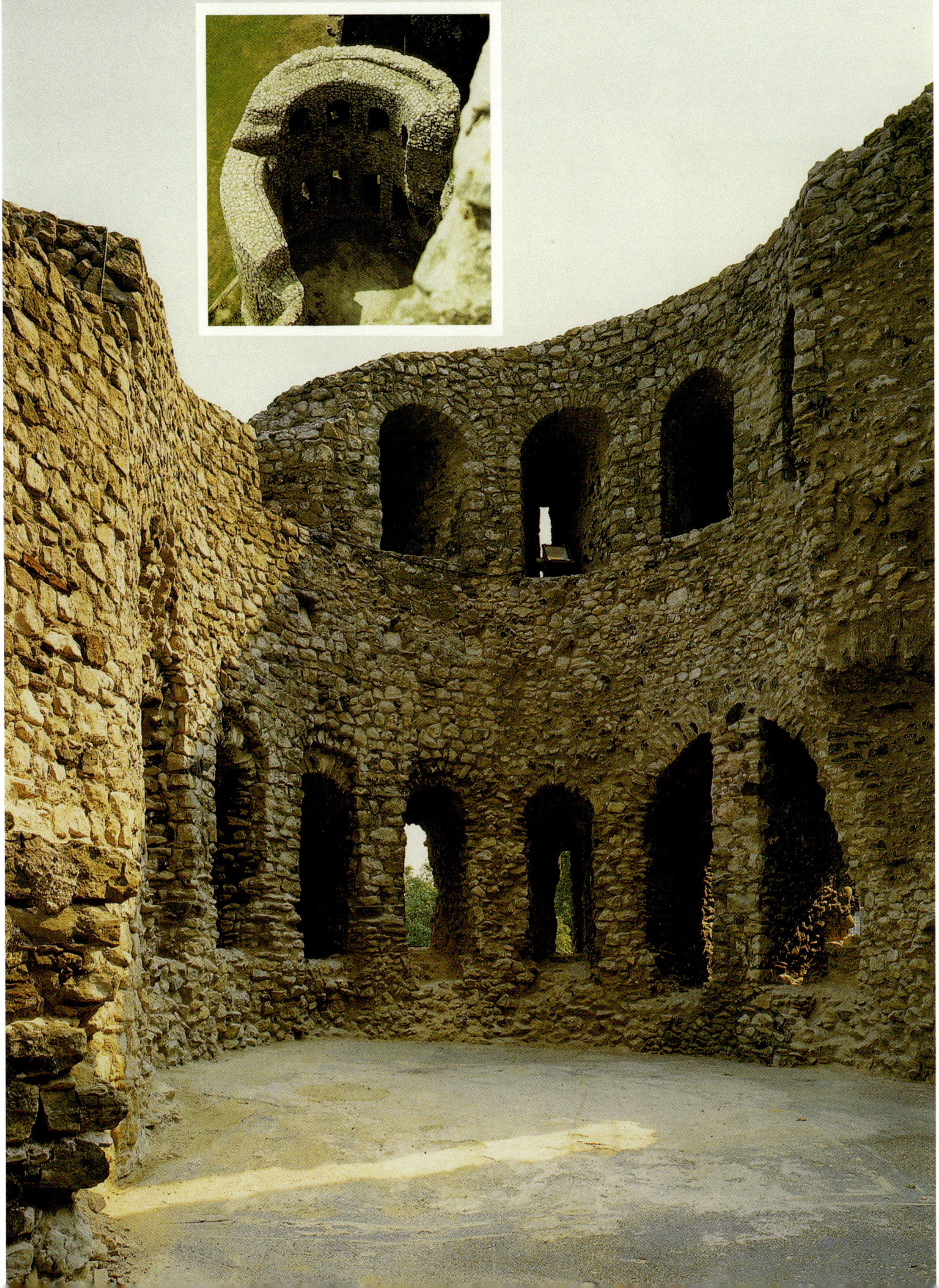

TOUR OF THE BAILEY

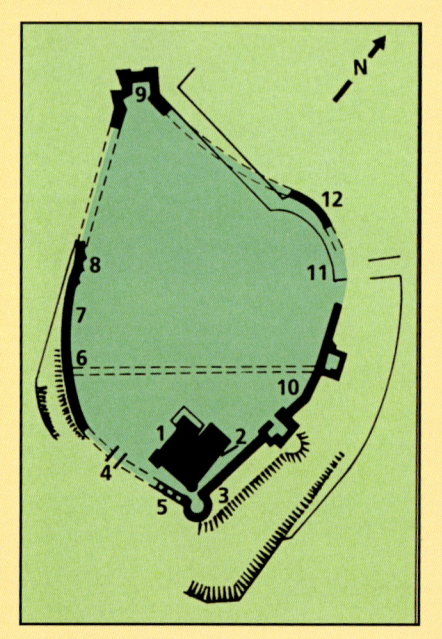

1. The keep
2. Postern door
3. Two-storey drum tower
4. Gate into bailey
5. South curtain wall
6. Embrasures in wall
7. River wall
8. Remnants of thirteenth-century building
9. Northwest bastion
10. Wall built by Edward III
11. Main outer gate
12. Part of Gundulf's wall

4 Go through the small gate. The south curtain wall was breached
5 by King John and rebuilt by Henry III. Note the arrow slits. The vertical line of stone near the broken left end probably marks one edge of the former south gate. The fissures down the south and east walls of the keep show clearly the destruction caused in John's siege. Though it was protected by the keep, this was the weakest side of the castle as it was vulnerable to attack from Boley Hill just behind.

6 Return to the bailey and note the four embrasures (splayed openings in a wall for admitting light or shooting through). These were possibly the windows of a thirteenth century building. From here a defensive wall once crossed the courtyard to the mural tower nearest the main gate. There must have been a gateway in this wall but its location is not known.

7 The river wall (and the south wall round to the drum tower) is Norman, though strengthened and raised by Henry III. The lower part is Gundulf's work. It rests on the old Roman city wall and is about 4ft (1.2m) thick at the base. Gundulf's masons used untrimmed stones, often laid aslant in herringbone fashion. At this point the line where the original wall was heightened in about 1250 can be seen clearly.

8 The remnants of another important thirteenth-century building were probably once part of a major residential complex. Note the three pointed vaults of the undercroft (basement or cellar), the line of holes above them for large floor joists, and the two fine windows (now blocked).

Right: **Curtain wall** at the west side of the bailey, showing traces of a hall built by Henry III against the wall

Fine late eleventh-century axehead Found in Rochester Castle ditch, this axehead is one of the most important pieces of evidence indicating that the original Norman castle was in the same areas as the present keep and bailey

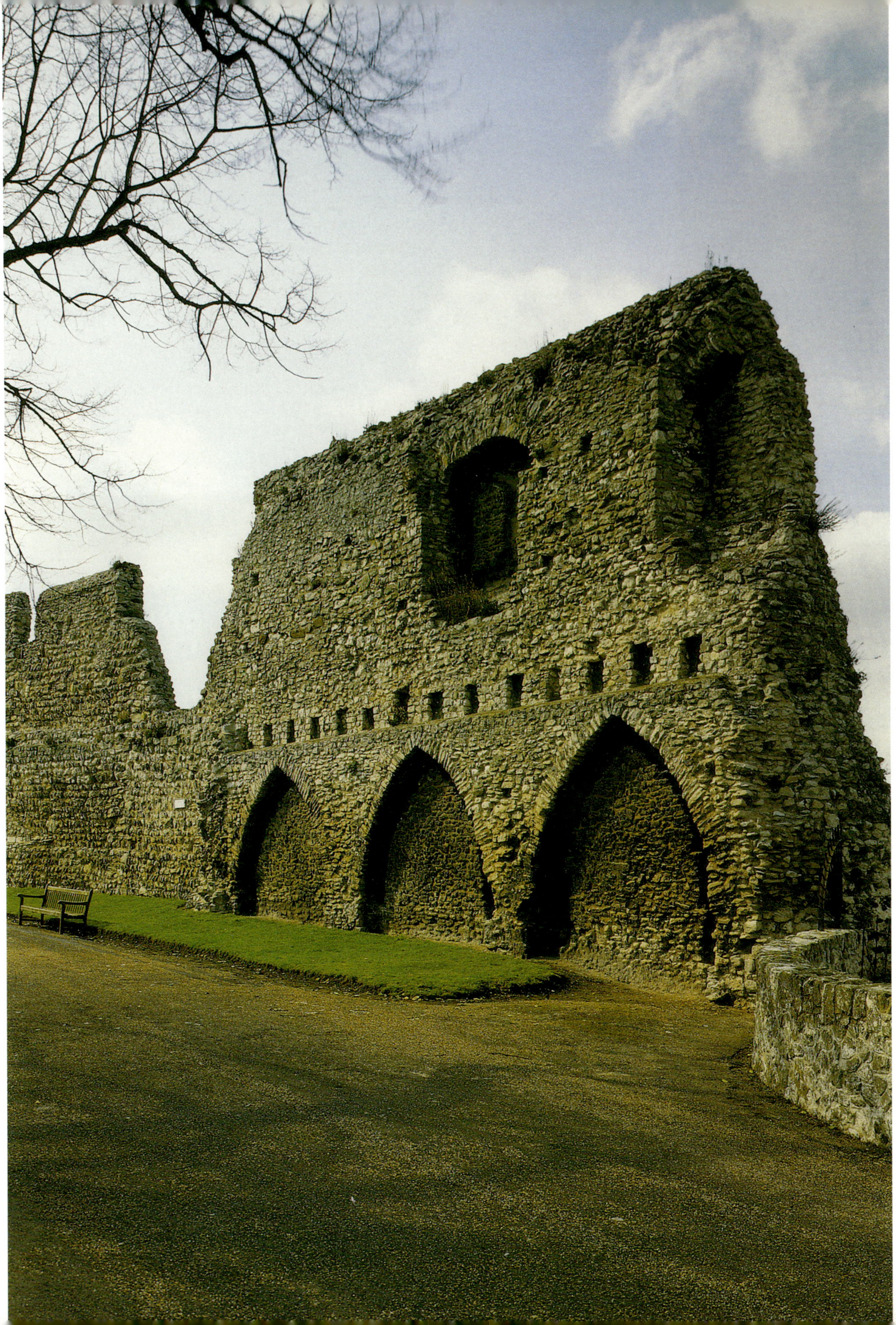

TOUR OF THE BAILEY

Entrance through the northwest bastion This was cut through Edward III's bastion in 1872 to give access to the new pleasure gardens in the bailey. The arch is decorated with chevrons in the style of the much older arches in the keep

9 The northwest bastion was built by Richard II about 1378–83. It controlled shipping on the river and also the main road that once passed close to its walls before crossing the old Rochester Bridge, some 250ft (76m) further upstream than the present bridge. There might once have been a small postern gate here but the present steps and entrance are modern. Though they imitate the Norman style with its chevron decoration, they were cut through in about 1872. The cannon is a relic of the Crimean War of 1854–56.

10 The section of wall from the southeastern drum tower to the main gate was rebuilt by Edward III around 1370. The tower on the right was part of Gundulf's castle; that on the left was built by Edward III. Through the gap in the wall between them, note the fine view of

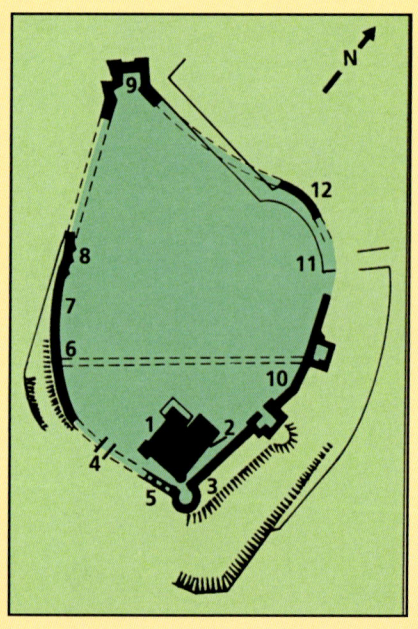

1 The keep
2 Postern door
3 Two-storey drum tower
4 Gate into bailey
5 South curtain wall
6 Embrasures in wall
7 River wall
8 Remnants of thirteenth-century building
9 Northwest bastion
10 Wall built by Edward III
11 Main outer gate
12 Part of Gundulf's wall

Reconstructed corner of the keep This had to be rebuilt after the siege of 1215. The rounded tower was designed to deflect missiles and it was inherently stronger than the original square towers

TOUR OF THE BAILEY

Rochester Cathedral and the width of the ditch. The ditch was always dry and was once much deeper, surrounding the castle on its three landward sides. Charles Dickens wanted to be buried in the graveyard later established here but was taken to Westminster Abbey instead.

11 The main outer gate was rebuilt about 1250 and further strengthened around 1370. The barbican of this powerful structure, including its drawbridge, would have stretched right across the ditch. It is shown in a dilapidated state in a drawing of 1717, but the last traces were demolished in 1870–72.

12 Across the road is another part of Gundulf's early Norman wall. Beyond it the gardens of the houses occupy what was once the ditch.

Square wall tower added to Gundulf's curtain wall in the fourteenth century

Rochester in 1717, Bridge Warden's map

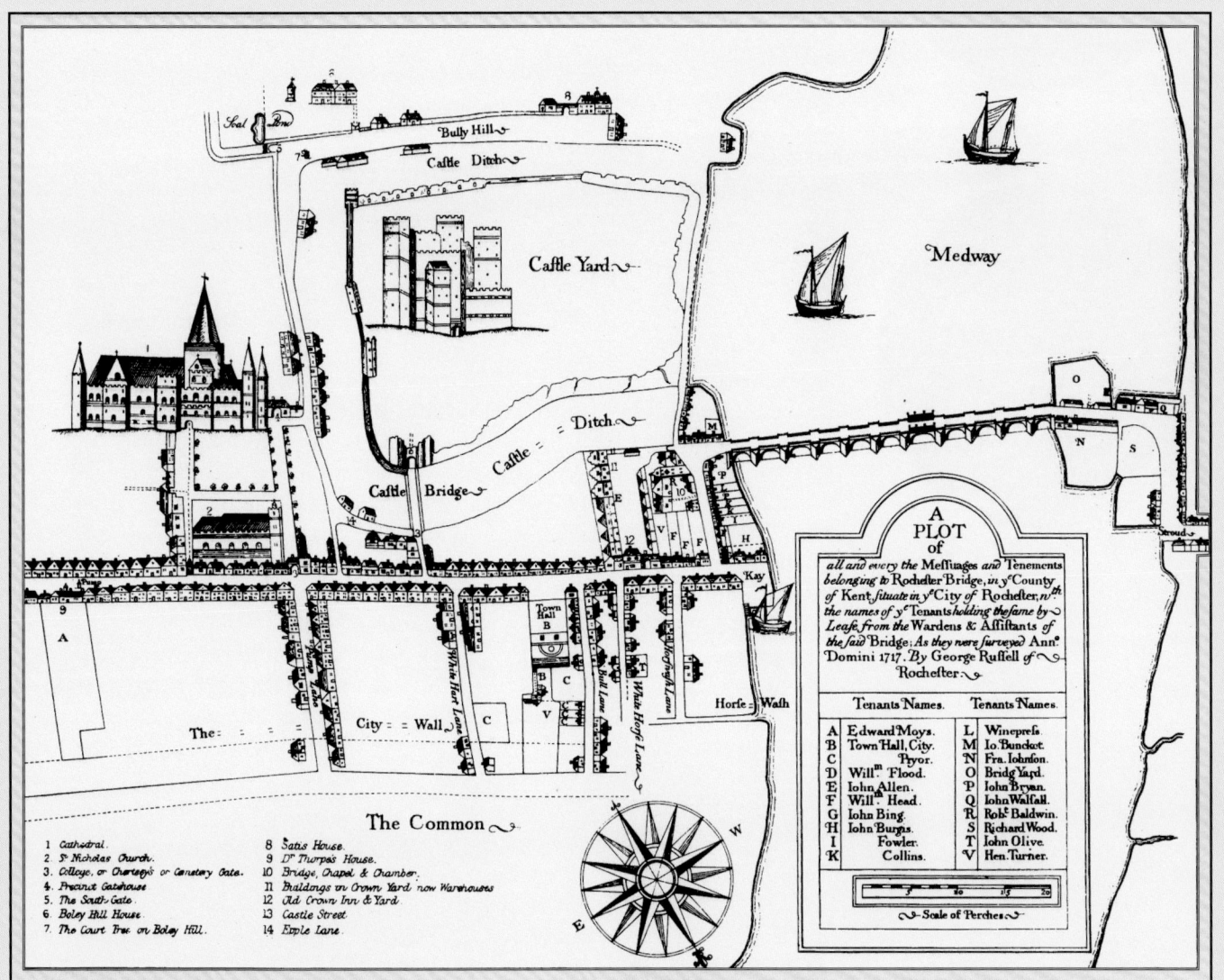

Rochester Castle at war

William I
(the Conqueror)

British Museum

William II
(Rufus)

Ashmolean Museum, Oxford

The Normans
The Normans inherited the restlessness, determination and potential for violence of their Viking forebears. Their government was based on feudalism, a complicated system of granting land in exchange for military service. Landless younger sons sought their fortunes by enlisting in the armies of other countries. By 1130 the Normans had set up states in southern Italy and Sicily as well as England.

Although common in northern France, castles were virtually unknown in England before the Norman Conquest. As the Normans worked their way across the country they consolidated their advance with fortifications from which to control the surrounding areas. In the early years these were often rough-and-ready affairs, put up quickly and made of wood. Many were of a type known as motte-and-bailey castles. The motte was a large mound of earth with a wooden keep on top. Beside it was a fortified enclosure called the bailey. Each was surrounded by a palisade and a wide ditch.

Siege!
During its history Rochester Castle underwent three important sieges:

1 **In May 1088** it was fortified against King William II by Odo, the quarrelsome Bishop of Bayeux and Earl of Kent. When William the Conqueror died in 1087 he left Normandy to his eldest son Robert and England to his second surviving son William. Odo led a conspiracy to put Robert on the throne but was besieged in Rochester by the King's army. Plagued by heat, flies and disease, the garrison was soon obliged to make terms and Odo went into exile. It may have been as a result of this incident that Gundulf was required to replace the wooden defences of Rochester Castle with new curtain walls of stone.

It used to be thought that Boley Hill, just outside the present walls, was the motte of the original castle. This is not now considered to be the case. Possibly it is in part a man-made earthwork constructed during this or subsequent sieges.

Norman soldiers before the battle of Hastings from a medieval manuscript

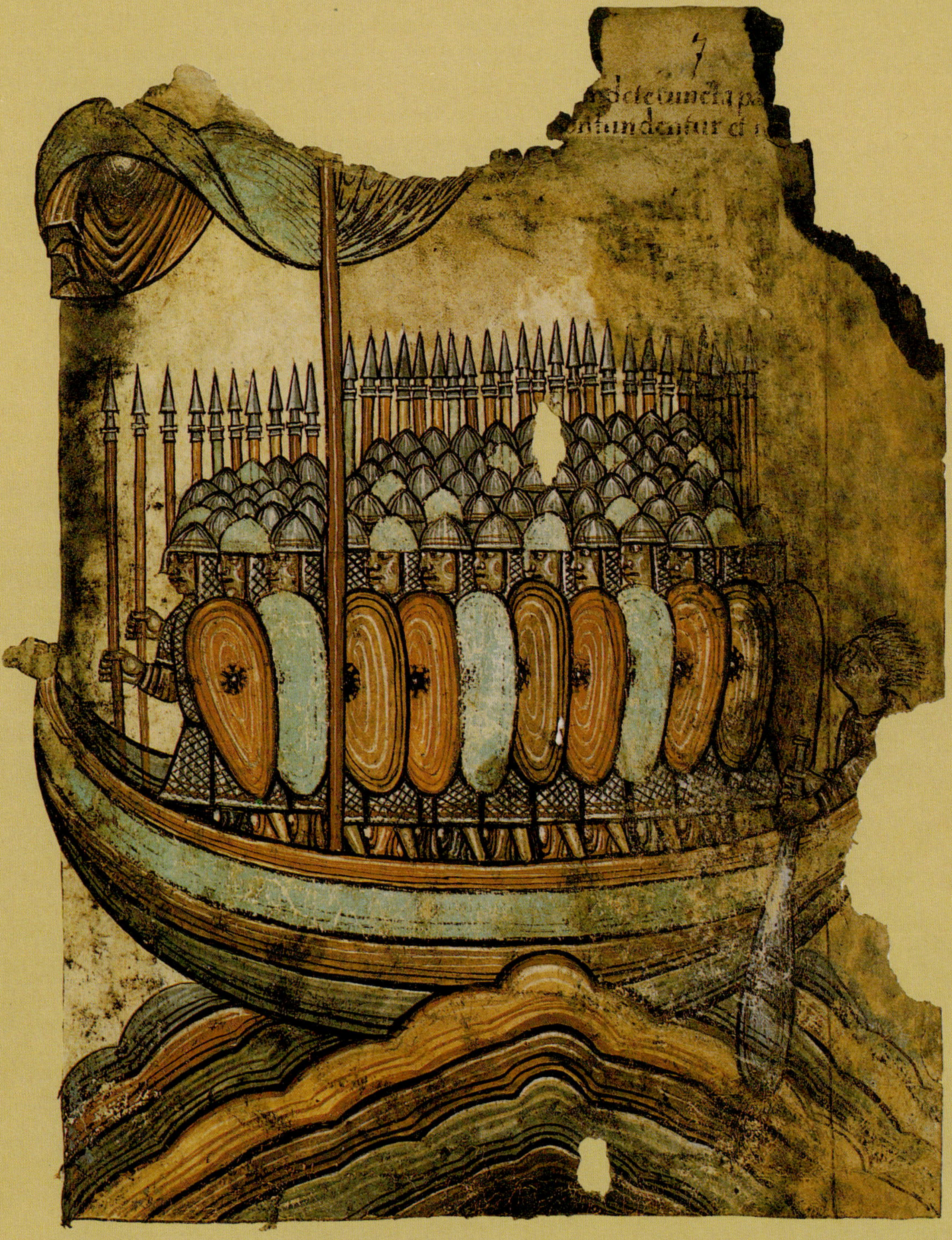

Bibliothèque Nationale, France

ROCHESTER CASTLE AT WAR

2   From 11 October to 30 November 1215 the castle was held for the barons against King John. Under the command of William de Albini and Reginald de Cornhill, some 95 to 140 knights (the historical accounts vary) defied the King for seven weeks.

John personally conducted a ferocious attack, battering at the walls with five stone-throwing machines from Boley Hill and keeping up a constant barrage of crossbow bolts. He breached the south curtain wall and drove the defenders back into the keep. Then his sappers undermined the southeast tower. When the tunnel was finished, the fat of forty pigs was used to burn through the pit-props and the collapse of these brought down a quarter of the keep.

Siege of 1215   King John leading an attack on Rochester Castle

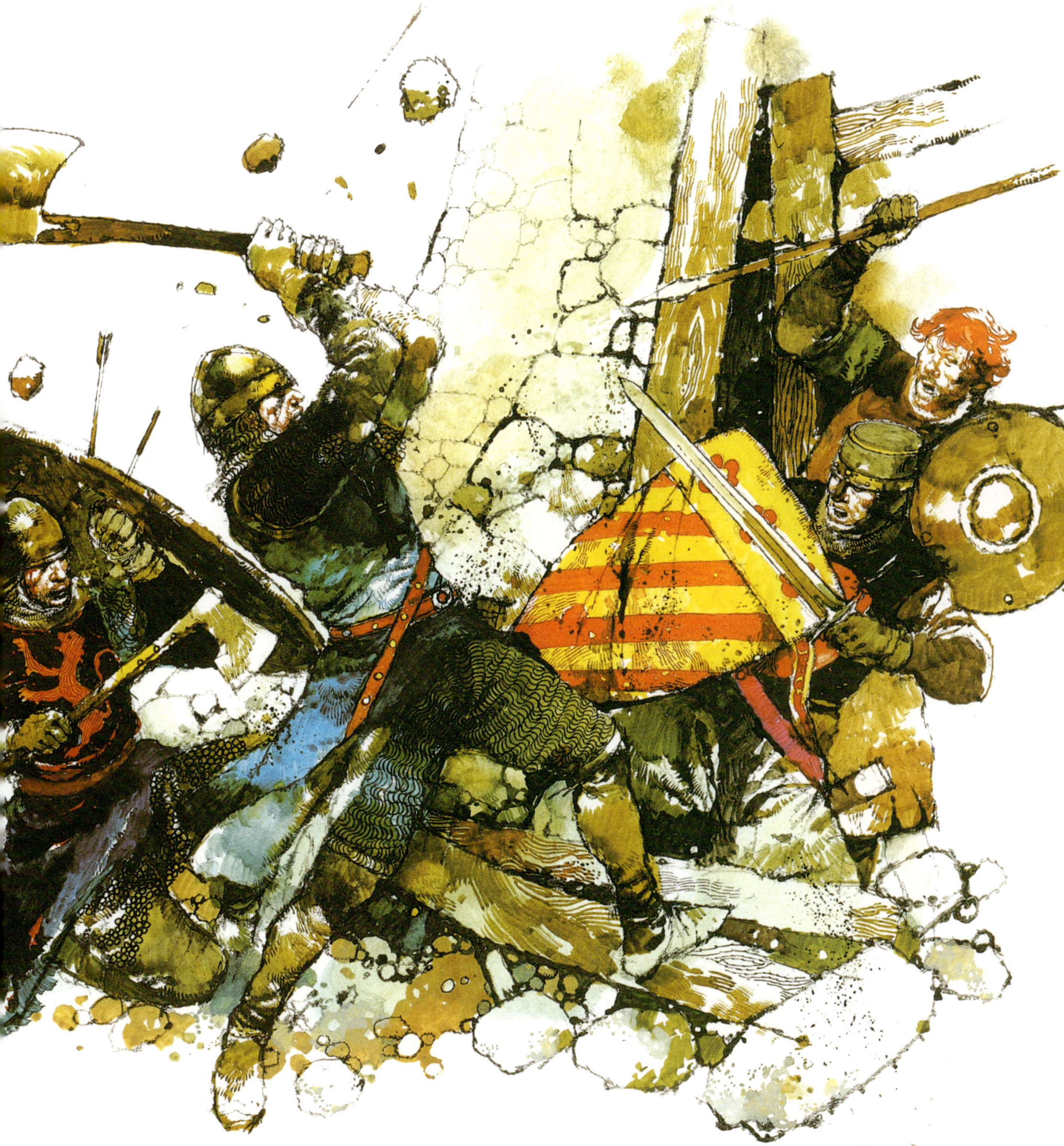

King John

Instruments like these were used to provide entertainment

Undaunted, and despite being reduced to a diet of horseflesh and water, the defenders retired behind the keep's cross wall and fought on in the ruins. Those who could no longer fight were sent out of the castle, some apparently to have their hands and feet lopped off on John's orders. Soon afterwards the remainder were forced to surrender when faced with starvation. 'Our age has not known a siege so hard pressed nor so strongly resisted,' wrote a chronicler. After that 'few cared to put their trust in castles.'

Infuriated by the determined defence, John intended to hang all those he had captured. One of his captains dissuaded him from this drastic reprisal for fear of retaliation, and he contented himself with imprisoning the rebel leaders at Corfe and elsewhere. He also took the castle into the custody of the Crown.

Repairs, 1220–60 Henry III, John's son, made the castle a major royal stronghold. Some £680 was spent over a twenty-year period, £530 of it on the keep. First the curtain walls were rebuilt or heightened. Then, around 1226, work began on repairing the shattered keep. A projecting drum tower was built to protect the vulnerable southeast corner of the bailey. Both this and the corner of the keep behind it were constructed in a cylindrical style to deflect missiles.

The main gateway was strengthened, and the now-vanished wall across the bailey may have been built at this time. Other important work was carried out on new residential accommodation, the chapels, an almonry and stables.

3 From 17–26 April 1264 the newly refurbished castle saw action during the Barons' War. In the fighting between Henry III and Simon de Montfort it was attacked by two rebel armies. Gilbert de Clare came up from his castle at Tonbridge, then the following day (Good Friday) de Montfort arrived from London.

Within twenty-four hours they had captured the outer bailey and forced the defenders under Roger de Leybourne back into the keep. A truce was declared on Easter Sunday but immediately afterwards the siege began in earnest. A week's battering by stone-throwing machines caused extensive damage to the keep with heavy casualties on both sides, and a mine tunnel was begun which would have brought about the castle's capture within another two days. However, de Montfort abandoned the siege when he heard that the King was approaching with a large army.

ROCHESTER CASTLE AT WAR

Repairs and works, 1367–83 The badly damaged castle was not repaired for over 100 years, by which time neglect and the 'great wind' of 1362 had added to the ruin. A survey by Edward III in 1363 put the cost of restoring it at the huge sum of £3333-6s-8d. Despite this, major reconstructions were put in hand to return the castle to its former power and by 1400 it had attained its maximum defensive capability.

Edward III repaired the keep, rebuilt whole sections of the walls and further strengthened the main gate, barbican and drawbridge. A few years later Richard II spent £500 providing the northern bastion to control the bridge over the River Medway. Rochester Bridge itself was also fortified and a drawbridge incorporated in the centre span.

Reconstructed corner of the keep The decorated Norman arches were not rebuilt in exactly the original size nor with such fine detail

Castle and community

The Normans built their castles to be strongpoints for their occupation and to overawe the surrounding area. In addition to being the home of a lord they also acted as tax-collecting points, courts and sometimes the local jail. Often they were whitewashed so they could be seen from a distance and impress their presence on the community.

The actual owner of a castle, in Rochester's case the Archbishop of Canterbury and later the King, did not usually live there permanently. He would visit from time to time as he journeyed round his various estates.

Mural tower and east curtain wall Built by Edward III 1367–70

Main outer gateway Rebuilt about 1250 and further strengthened around 1370 by Edward III. With its stone causeway leading over the ditch to the town, this whole structure protected the main entrance to the castle

Large outer bailey This enclosure provided the place of work and accommodation for the brewer, blacksmith, armourer, carpenters, masons, stablehands, cooks, washerwomen, horses, hawks and hunting dogs. It would also have provided an arena for outdoor sports and contests

Ditch around the bailey Deep and quite an obstacle to would-be attackers

Northwest bastion This protected the bailey and keep from attack on the river side. Built by Richard II (1378–83) it dominated the medieval bridge over the Medway and controlled shipping

New buildings, repairs and alterations were in progress until late medieval times when the castle was abandoned

Note how impenetrable the keep and bailey must have been. With the river running down one side of the bailey, the ditch protecting the other three sides and battlemented walls and towers covering all vulnerable places, the castle was designed to protect those inside by deterring potential attackers

Forebuilding The purpose of this was to protect the entrance to the keep. It was itself protected by a guard tower, a drawbridge and a pit 9ft wide and 15ft deep (2.7 by 4.6m). A portcullis that could be lowered between the forebuilding and the keep gave additional protection

Mural tower Built by Edward III on the site of an early twelfth-century tower

Keep Built in the years following 1127 by Archbishop William de Corbeil, the keep was both military strong-point and prestigious accommodation for its owners

Battlements From here the surrounding countryside and river could be surveyed and enemies attacked

Joist holes Projecting covered platforms were erected (see page 12) from which an enemy reaching the base of the keep could be attacked

Guard tower This enabled an initial check to be made on visitors

Cross wall This provided another line of defence

Inner bailey

Alan Sorrell

Rochester Castle as it might have appeared in the fifteenth century

CASTLE AND COMMUNITY

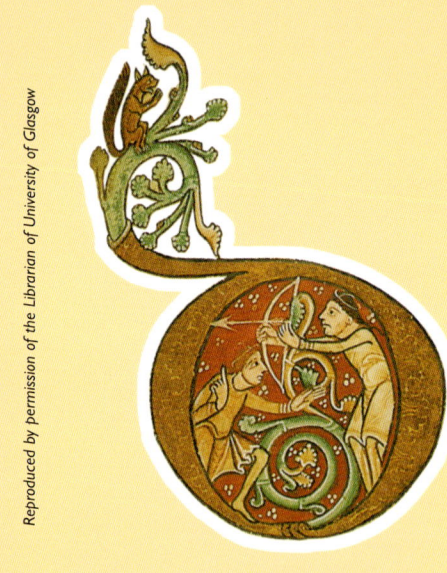

Illuminated manuscripts Decorations from contemporary religious manuscripts

Everyday affairs were supervised by a resident constable who saw to the maintenance of the fabric and the administration of the area. Under him was the steward who acted as a kind of general manager. There would be a few knights who had the obligation of performing forty days' castle-guard service in exchange for their lands, but unless under threat of attack the garrison was small, probably only a dozen or so.

Life in an early Norman castle was not as glamorous as films and television often suggest. Even for the nobility it could be cold, dirty and uncomfortable. There was no glass in the windows, and rushes were laid on the floors. Woven or embroidered hangings were sometimes put round the doors and walls to try to exclude draughts and keep rooms warmer. In winter everyone huddled round open fires or braziers which caused so much smoke that interior walls had to be whitewashed every spring. Splendour and squalor went hand in hand.

The bailey was not the pleasant expanse of grass it is now. According to the season it could have been an expanse of mud or dust, full of the workshops of tradesmen such as blacksmiths and armourers, carpenters, masons, stablehands, cooks, washerwomen and brewers. In addition there were horses, hunting dogs and hawks.

Light was at a premium in most medieval buildings, so throughout the year the working day began at dawn and ended at twilight. Try to imagine how gloomy the lower rooms at Rochester were when the floors were in place, the only illumination coming from tiny windows and homemade candles or rushlights. At higher levels, window seats were used to make the most of all available daylight.

The centre of a castle's life was the Constable's Hall. Here most of the estate's everyday business was conducted, rents were paid, local courts were held. It was also the place where those who lived in the castle ate. Most people owned nothing but the clothes they stood up in and the knife at their belt. There was very little privacy. The lord and his lady had a hall and chamber of their own, and a few lucky individuals might share a small private room or cubbyhole. But by and large everyone slept on benches or on mattresses on the floors of public rooms and corridors, wrapped in their cloaks.

Furniture was rudimentary, consisting mainly of chests, stools, benches and trestle tables which could be cleared away when not required. The only high-backed chair in the castle might be that of the lord at the great table at one end of the hall.

Meals were eaten together, with the highest to the lowest seated in strict order of rank. Breakfast was early but was not much more than a hunk of bread, with a more substantial morning meal being taken at 10 or 11 o'clock. Dinner was in the late afternoon and in summer a light supper would precede bed.

Top right: **The king or lord** would inspect building work with his surveyor

Right: **Craftsmen and labourers** at work on a building

Offa rex

Peasants working on the land produced the landowners' wealth that enabled manor houses and castles to be built

Decoration from a contemporary illuminated manuscript

Beef, pork, veal or mutton formed a major part of the diet, though venison was a royal prerogative. As there were few plates and no forks, meat was served up on slices of bread called trenchers and eaten with the fingers. Huge numbers of chickens and geese were consumed, and thousands of eggs. Fish and eels were also greatly sought after. There was not much available in the way of green vegetables - mainly cabbages, onions and leeks; potatoes were unknown.

In the winter, animals kept for food were slaughtered because of lack of fodder, and the castle filled its storerooms with cured bacon, hams, and barrels of salted meat and fish. Dried peas and beans would be used to make soups. Butter and cheese were made locally. The main beverages were ale and wine which were stored in the buttery in great casks, so although the well was important it was not necessarily a critical factor during a siege.

Important additions to meals, especially for the top table, were piquant sauces made from spices and herbs. These helped to liven up bland food or disguise the taste of salted meat. Spices often had to be imported from abroad and were kept under lock and key as they were very expensive. Those most commonly used were pepper, ginger,

CASTLE AND COMMUNITY

cinnamon and nutmeg, with herbs such as parsley, sage, garlic, fennel and borage.

Kitchens were usually kept well away from living accommodation for fear of fire. There is no sign of one in the keep at Rochester, so probably it was in a separate building in the bailey. This meant that food could be nearly cold by the time it reached the hall, although meat was often boiled and carried into the keep in its cauldron. Other food could be reheated over braziers.

Hygiene was virtually nonexistent. There were no washing facilities apart from bowls of water. Latrines would discharge into a cesspit at the base of a tower or simply vent to the outside to trickle down the walls. Both types can be found at Rochester.

Before very long the spartan living conditions associated with the old Norman keeps were no longer acceptable, and by the second half of the twelfth century any new castle that was built attached considerable importance to comfort. In the older castles, such as Rochester, the lord and his principal officials moved out of the keep into new residential suites that were constructed in the bailey and possessed the civilised amenities in keeping with a more settled way of life.

Garderobe (latrine) chutes which discharged on the east side of the keep

Chronology of Rochester

1066	Battle of Hastings; accession of William the Conqueror
?1067–70?	Construction of first castle in timber
1086	Castle mentioned in Domesday Book
May 1088	First siege of the castle during rebellion of Norman barons under Odo, Bishop of Bayeux
c1088	Timber defensive fencing and buildings (except the keep) rebuilt in stone by Gundulf, Bishop of Rochester
1127	Castle placed in the custody of the Archbishop of Canterbury
c1127	Construction of the present keep by Archbishop William de Corbeil
1172–73	Henry II spent £100 on the castle during his sons' rebellion
1206	King John spent £115 on the castle's defences
1215	King John forced to sign Magna Carta
October to November 1215	Second siege of the castle by King John; destruction of the southeast corner of the keep; custody of the castle reclaimed by the Crown
1220–60	Repairs and improvements to the castle costing £680 (£530 of it on the keep) plus a further £300 to provide a deep ditch around the city
April 1264	Third siege of the castle by Simon de Montfort during the Barons' War
1264–1367	Castle neglected
1300	Visit by Edward I during a progress through Kent
1314	Queen Isabel of Scotland, wife of Robert Bruce, was a prisoner in the castle for several months
1367–83	Extensive repairs and rebuilding under Edward III and Richard II, including construction of northern bastion, 1378–83
1381	Castle attacked during Peasants' Revolt
1383–93	Rochester Bridge rebuilt in stone (demolished by gunpowder in 1857)
1416	Visit by Sigismund, Emperor of Germany, with a retinue of 1000 knights
1492	First of three visits by Henry VII
1522	Visit by Henry VIII and Charles V, Emperor of Germany
1540	Henry VIII went to Rochester to meet his fourth wife, Anne of Cleves, for the first time
c1500–1600	Progressive neglect and deterioration; keep burnt out
1610	James I gave the castle to Sir Anthony Weldon, in whose family it remained until the nineteenth century; stone and timber sold off to local builders
1780	Abortive proposal for the castle to be purchased by the government for use as barracks; further proposals to demolish the castle entirely abandoned because of difficulty and expense
1870	Castle grounds leased from the Earl of Jersey by the City of Rochester and turned into a public pleasure garden
1870–72	Last traces of medieval outer gate and drawbridge demolished; new entrance cut through northwest bastion
1884	Purchase of freehold by City of Rochester for £6572
1965	Responsibility for the castle taken over by the Ministry of Public Building and Works (later the Department of the Environment)
1984	English Heritage took over responsibility for the castle

The front cover shows the keep viewed from the castle gardens. The back cover shows the round south-east tower, which replaced the one destroyed by King John in 1215